Death, Contagion, and Unnatural Sleep

POEMS

Tyler Deaton

FIRST EDITION, **Spring 2025**
LIBRARY OF CONGRESS CARD CATALOG NUMBER: *pending*
ISBN 978-1-965784-06-8 HARDBACK
ISBN 978-1-965784-03-7 PAPERBACK

Cover Graphic Design & Book Typography by Kurt Lovelace.
Cover artwork by PIERIAN SPRINGS PRESS.
Cover type *Bauhaus Dessau* **Alfarn** by Céline Hurka,
Elia Preuss, Flavia Zimbardi,
Hidetaka Yamasaki, and Luca Pellegrini.
Author name, blurbs, footers in **Jenson** by Robert Slimbach.
Back cover description in **Gill Sans Nova**.
Titles and body text set in **Baskerville**.
Flourishes set in Emigre Foundry **Dalliance** by Frank Heine.
Emigre Foundry **ZeitGuys** by Bob Aufuldish, Eric Donelan.
Typefaces licensed Adobe, Linotype, Emigre, & URW GmbH.

PSPRESS.PUB
PIERIAN SPRINGS PRESS, INC
30 N GOULD ST, STE 25398
SHERIDAN, WYOMING 82801-6317

For Mark & Tammi
To whom I owe everything

CONTENTS

Six By Infinity

Part I

A Night In Venice

One 3

Two 4

Three 6

Obi, ... 7

Five 8

Six 9

Seven 10

Tyler, ... 12

Part II

Postcards To Somewhere

Part III

Down by the Creek

i 27

Spin Cycle 28

ii 29

Grey is the New Grey 30

iii 31

Fine Dining after a Draught from Rip's Flagon 32

iv 34

A Bed of Bees 35

v 36

It's Fine 37

vi 39

Call Me Bonzo 40

Part IV

Letters To Somewhere

Part V

Unnatural Sleep

Canvas of the Big Bang 55

Minute Maid Cadence 56

What do we say to the god of death? 58

Risk Assessment 60

Confection Sprinkled with Love 62

A friendly summertime 63

A Red Pill 64

The Art of Going Green 65

The Forever Spring Break 67

Pneumonoultramicroscopicsilicovolcanoconiosis 69

Stocking up on the Essentials 70

Playing for the Ruins 71

Death, Contagion & Unnatural Sleep 72

Gee Brain, what are we gonna do tonight? 73

The Art of Going Extinct 75

A Case for Icarus 77

When Hamlet has Insomnia 80

Estimated Time of Arrival 83

PART VI

SOMEWHERE

V.   Trauma Counselor 87

IV. Backseat Driver 90

III. American Dreamer 95

II. Motivational Runner 99

I. Trauma Counselor 102

Notes   105

Acknowledgments   108

About the Author   109

"I hear some noise. Lady, come from that nest
Of death, contagion, and unnatural sleep.
A greater power than we can contradict
Hath thwarted our intents."

William Shakespeare
Romeo And Juliet
Act 5, Scene 3, 151-154

Death, Contagion, Unnatural Sleep

Six by Infinity

Wrapping paper confetti, wish list essential,
you & I exchange weighted blankets.

Waving UV wands, fogging Plexiglas shields,
the subtitles in our eyes read: you get me.

Discarding sacks of memories, smoking rose petals
    along the walkway,
your thought bubble populates: what does it mean to get me?

Dusting a top-shelf whiskey, teetering a hand-me-down chair,
I wrap myself in six feet of silence.

Embedding ash in the porous concrete, honeybees dropping
    on the curb,
this is where one of us soliloquies this is nothing new.

Sagging rock-n-roll T-shirts, spooning memory-foam pillows,
your intertitle flashes: god, let a touch release oxytocin.

Stagnating breaths in the sheetrock, shattering records
    against the vanity mirror,
I too ask to be scripted as feeling something.

Stage ropes extending from the ceiling, bristles
    hugging our necks, & we
kick the chairs for a tighter embrace.

I

A NIGHT IN VENICE

A thing of beauty is a joy forever:
Its loveliness increases; it will never
Pass into nothingness.

John Keats
ENDYMION: A POETIC ROMANCE
BOOK 1, LINES 1-3

One

Obi refrains from using the word—bored. The man, it once accompanied, quoted Berryman often. Muttered more like it: *Life, friends, is boring. We must not say so.* How the Venetian lamp posts mock Obi for being a shadow without an object to follow. All their flickering spectacle against the Istrian stone. But Obi had such a promising man to follow! The way he burst into that monster commune (O yes, monsters exist), & stomped on the Earth Monster's garden, then tussled with a shapeshifter. But it's always the same: brave face, weak heart. If only Obi had read him better. A few charades. A little haunting—should have inspired panic not madness. But after destroying the monster commune, how the man wandered through the woods, cross countries, cross canals, the plaza, up the steps of St. Mark's Campanile, then jumped. It should've known.   *I always wanted to be old, I wanted to say*

(.. ..-. / -.-- --- ..- / ..-. --- -.-. ..- ...)

Two

The concerto is at the Chiesa di San Vidal. My cousin, opposed
to chamber, decides her evening culture shall come from an
Amarone. She snatches the map, leaves me near the church's
door, crosses the canal, heads toward the hotel bar—

The program says we'll be dining on the 18th century
masterpieces of Antonio Vivaldi. I ease into the audience. To
think, their centuries of music versus America's decades. How
we hunger to slip through time.

We cheer for an encore, and the cellist abides. O how the music
entwines with his movements, emotion with his strings. The
violins and bassist sit idly in his shadow.

10:30 pm. We shuffle across the bridge, the melodies still
imprinted on us. They cross another bridge, and I turn right,
certain the hotel is just beyond.

Traveling 101: without providing your cellular provider your
itinerary, your iPhone, across seas, is useless.

After thirty minutes pass, the only thing I've discovered is a
need to pee.

Don't panic—just another bridge, just another turn.

English? Do you know English?

All the kiosks are closed.

Conosco un po

It's amazing how pressure,

on your bladder, can

exacerbate your

nerves.

Three

The man never even twitched when his body hit the cobblestones. Why should Obi feel fault for this? The man entered that monster commune searching for death. A few shadowy charades were not the push. Obi wishes they had toured St. Mark's Basilica beforehand—the four bronze horses at the entrance, the arches, the murals. The monsters loathed art enough to adamantly burn everything in the commune. There had been a Lamia, who cherished & discussed Greek mythos. But Obi signs to communicate, & followed a tawny cat at the time, which had no digits. *In sight of a more peaceful country, just beyond*—Some tourist is bound to discover the man with blood pooling around his ears. This Obi is certain of. There'll be screams, & flash photography, & whistles, & sneakers, or loafers, or stilettos, if lucky, & it'll finally stretch through the Basilica.

(If you focus, you'll notice the Venetian lamp posts
 flicker Morse code)

Obi,

If you focus, you'll notice the Venetian lamp posts flicker Morse code: Do you crave that chaos? Not really. That many bodies moving at cross-purposes—overloads a shadow. It's no surprise you've muddled your desires, your makeup just the imprints of the shoes you inhabit. The first man you followed believed, "a thing of beauty is a joy forever." That's why you hunger for art. Sadly, your memory seems as ephemeral as your shape. The reason you haunt—maybe the second had a penchant for jesting. Fear not: you'll either slip into nothingness or affix yourself to something more temperate.

Best of Luck,
Mr. Deaton

Five

1:30 am. The map directs me back to the abandoned train
station. No

that hasn't happened yet. I am lost

in a forest, while picking blackberries. Thought I could race
Paw Paw back home. Thorns, from the briar, snag my shirt, my
ankles, my wrists. Whoa

that's too far back. In 1433 Cosimo de' Medici is exiled to
Venice for the capital crime "of having to sought to elevate
himself higher than others." A wrong

turn here. And another there. Across this canal, the lights
remind me of lunching with my cousin in Murano, of watching
blown glass. Needle nosed pliers pulled a molten rod into a
horse. Coincidentally, we also ate pizza topped with shredded
horse. The meat a little tough. Wrong

direction; the hotel is inside Venice. 12:30 am.

Another hotel, another lobby. A helpful concierge loans me a
map, circles the correct hotel.

Most of the street names in Venice have been worn off the
buildings by time. The roads
themselves, arch

and fragment. In 1737 the last of the Medici family died.

A horse would have a better sense of direction.

Six

This is quick. The Polizia glance up, glance down, have the man shoved in a bag, dragged off somewhere, have the cobblestones hosed, and that is that. Not a wasted step. Not a stray stiletto. They manage to cleanse the streets, but a shadow of the event lingers. What Obi would give for a cat. How can it enjoy the city's mystique stuck to the edge of a building? Is that a rat? No, just a coffee cup hobbling across the plaza. If only the man's heart hadn't broken—it was like braille over his soles. What can you do with a man like that? Luckily, sunrise will come soon enough, the tourist packing in with all their unresolved traumas. Hopefully there will be an artist—soul tortured enough to haunt, but work enough to finish. Burning all that art, those monsters didn't comprehend. *It's*
wonderful the way cats bound about

(Tyler, holding a map, meanders toward the shadow)

Seven

When stumbling across the abandoned train station, a pressured bladder exacerbates my panic. It's all: Would police patrol a defunct transport? Would homeless spring from the shadows?

Wrong turn, and another. Is that

me, in the reflection of a compartment window, chunking a map?

 2:15 am. Couples mingle outside the bars—*Do you know where this is?*

I admit, during some part of the night, there are high walls, a few bushes, no people. It's the only way to think—

Maybe if I grab a map from another hotel. *Just follow right there.*

It's strange to think this city is steadily sinking.

The second time my feet step toward that station, curiosity trumps anxiety. Wired fences. Graffiti on the bricks. Overgrown grass. Pass a decrepit platform, is a low wall and a modern street. Botts' dots. Is that a Ferrari? Did my shadow morph into hand puppets—of a hatchet? That morning, my cousin and I cut/skipped/ overslept a wine tasting to tour Scuola Grande of San Rocco. The Sistine Chapel of Venice. If I was a poet—suffice it to say wealthy citizens commissioned Tintoretto to decorate the building. 1564. Is that it? Everything

looks the same at night. Peeing in public is improper; losing your Paw Paw's heirloom in a forest—is that condemnable?

There is a building, just outside of Piazza Saint Marco, that James Bond sunk with a couple of bullets. Espionage speeding time along.

Hemingway once wrote that Venice is a labyrinth.

At the bottom of the map, written in English, reads: please flip over—

Tyler,

Now, you know Hemingway really compared Venice to a cross-word puzzle, that he'd have strolled these streets all his life, but anxiety has you swapping facts. Originally, the map should have escorted you to the hotel lobby by 2:30, a breath before your cousin dials the Polizia, then clock churning, you should have boarded a train for Florence, the birthplace of the Renaissance —beheld what the Medici's helped elevate, but you stepped on a shadow. This inauspicious revision has memories resurfacing: you running through a forest, you hacking briar patches with a hatchet, losing the hatchet, your Paw Paw nearly losing it when he finds you. Should you have known his Paw Paw carved the handle? Or that he'd drop from heat exhaustion searching for that heirloom? Does Obi blame you? Let's detour away from this line of inquiry. It's true—a shadow lingers on this memory, but can there be beauty in how you repurpose it? Fear not: we can incinerate this line of inquiry as well: either inhabit the cultural beauty, or tread over the same cobblestones, fixating on that expired train station, sinking in guilt.

Best of Luck,
Mr. Deaton

II

POSTCARDS TO SOMEWHERE

Evelyn,

Ryan & I drove by the old house on blocks. Remember it? Only holidays we made the drive was Easter, so maybe not. It's quite the eye sore now—pistons hang from the gutters, mushrooms burgeon from a tree stump. Still, I'd hoped to show Ryan my roots, but then Aunt Marg, while sipping an old fashioned, started cussing servants that left decades ago, which has me wondering if holidays stopped there b/c it had become unsafe (like they claim), or if it'd always been that way.

If you ever stop by, don't mention moving. For her, there's something about spongy floorboards that makes this home.

Rosaline

Sorry,

So that's Ryan in the last pic. If y'all meet, ask him about S.B.; you'll die.

Also, humor me? Every Easter, we hunted eggs (you must remember). The aunts hid them all over—hummingbird feeder to well pump. One year, I remember being determined to capture the most. Oh & slipping a lot (must've rained that morning). The same year, you went for a golden egg in the fig tree, your saddle shoes slipping too, a tiny branch harpooning your leg. Aunt Marg drove you to the hospital. Multiple stitches. When I brought it up, she just shook her head. Dialed mom, & her silence shook too. It happened, right?

You must tell me next holiday,

Rosaline

Evelyn,

Missed you Thanksgiving. No one knew if work or illness kept you.

After the Marg fiasco, I had to show Ryan our first house. Told him you were only nine months when we moved. Is nine months enough to qualify somewhere as home? Everything was how I remember—except the cul-de-sac was wrapped in cellophane. Actually when we slit the plastic, I noticed concrete where the rose bush had been. Oh & boards over everyone's windows. Strange, right? Hurricane season had passed (I checked my app). I had hoped we'd tour my roots, but even the front-porch mats & door bells were piled in the center, ready to burn. He seemed let down, & though I didn't tell him, I was too. That's just the past, I guess.

Hope this postcard reaches you well,

Rosie

~~Dear Dad,~~
I---

Sorry, Ryan must've scribbled on this before realizing it's a postcard. Almost forgot these were in a drawer too. Before you were born, we traveled most holidays. Mom collecting postcards, dad collecting shot glasses. The bar in the picture is Hemingway's. Key West, not Cuba. Which was his exile? While in the gift shop, I remember this man in a neon-orange speedo running down Duval St. Maybe a parade? Oh did you know the bars don't close till four? Shouting outside the hotel door taught me that. You & I should plan a trip soon. Not somewhere in the past, but somewhere new. Cuba's open, right?

Rosie

Should I talk to Ryan about his letter?

~~Evelyn,~~
O Evie,

Are these finding you? The news said postal services are suspended. They preached to stay indoors, but never why. Typical parenting—only relaying what they think you need to know. You must think me silly writing this way. Remember when we snuck letters under the door b/c one of us was grounded? Truth is, I lost your number some time ago, &—

Ryan's been stocking up on toilet paper & beer, but won't say why. Significant others, parents. I asked if he wanted to see the hospital where I was born, but he said it wasn't safe. As if we were some contagion to be quarantined. Cooped up in this living room, I keep thinking of those knockout roses. They really were the crème of spring. Such a shame mom let them die.

Please write,

Rosie

~~Dear Dad,~~
~~Ho~~

So now I write between Ryan's silences. Sorry if the message is cramp. You'd think with how taciturn he can be these letters would be expansive, but postcards are limiting by nature. Lately nature is limiting. How I miss not sleeping b/c my back had harnessed the sun. Blisters on my toes from the sand. Hell, I miss just walking to the convenience store. You know the nutritional value of toilet pap-
~~Do you remember when we went camping?~~
er? I will say this house has more character than I remember. Turning a light on in the living room, turns the lights off in the master. The acoustics in the foyer create perfect pitch when you scream. O Evie,

Evie,

How am I to fill time tethered to one spot? Originally thought maybe this would be a time to revisit my checklist: get in marathon shape, draft a business plan with no overhead. Certain internet searches have started bringing up the message: do you really wanna know? Maybe chuck out all the childhood junk stashed in the guest room. Maybe replace the hyacinth that died last summer. Started walking toward the neighborhood park to network, but instead binged Netflix. Maybe discover a parallel universe. Maybe learn *tree,* so I can implore them to stop self-combusting (that's how it works, right?). Started a holistic diet, but *we got this* won't grow on the balcony. Maybe—So my mind is trapped on a treadmill. There Sis, I said it.

Evie,

I'm beginning to understand the one-sided nature of this exchange: a picture shows where I've been, a message maybe of where I'd like to go, but there's no space for you. I promise this is NOT just an attempt to bottle sanity. This tethering is like an unnatural sleep. Why last night I dreamt we went to the carnival during rodeo. You won a giant stuffed bear for inventing a new deep-fried dessert or for spading the mechanical bull (forget which). We went inside this funhouse (the one with all the mirrors), & the bear got angry seeing itself, broke all the glass. This morning, a bed of bees lined the driveway. What's it all mean? I'd trade answers for a hug at this point.

Wish I could slide this under your door,

Sis

O Sis,

I finally caved & asked mom for your number, but your voicemail's full.

There's strange sounds at night. I keep telling myself it's solicitors, or god-forbid bears (yes, neither are native). I asked Ryan if he wanted to smell the sheets where I was conceived, but he never looked up from the radio. Sometimes I feel he's learned all he cares to about me. Sometimes the sofa smells of those roses. Remember that house? I pray not. Mom & dad fought so often then. In the house. In the car: *how about that girl? She's cute. You going to screw her too?*

Ryan won't board the windows, b/c I can't survive without sunshine. That's a small mercy, right? I wish we could get in touch. Those days really felt like the end of the world.

Love,
Your Sis

III

DOWN BY THE CREEK

i

Under the sun, June heat sops up the creek and exhumes
    vertebrae of red clay.
Under the sun, puddles trap bass and ripple the buzz
    of June bugs.

Jimmy drives a Firebird with sunroof shut as thirst seeps
    through the air vent.
Before happy hour, he mows our lawn. Mowing connects him
    to the heat.

Thirty percent chance of rain all week, weatherman says.
    Spray trucks suit up.
Mosquito eggs await thunder while the clay cracks.

With hydration packs strapped, hikers and bikers
    wear trails to sand.
Neither expects treads to slip in sand. From trail
    to bank, twenty-foot drop.

When Jimmy was a child, a lawnmower severed three of his toes.
Can toes long for feet? Is longing an impulse wired?

Frigyes Karinthy fabricated the six degrees of separation
    in a 1929 short story.
I strive for relationships, but the tenuous connections crumble.

Spin Cycle

You have a secret under your skin. You Mr. Roboto now? your pops asks. You, not knowing Styx, simply say, you're not a Roomba. When your pops suggests you need Jesus, you consult the four pillars of your faith: Wiki, Twitter, Insta & Tumblr. How that holy-blue light washes over your face, providing a vision of another swallowing a Tide Pod. Well that was that. From the laundry room, you snag a detergent capsule, let the plastic (nay the communion) slide against your tonsils, then wait for the secret to be cleansed. When nothing happens, you begin to spin, which causes your face to blot, your joints to uncouple,

>   your head to tumble up to your mother's foot.

Oh, there's my purple balaclava, she says. She plucks the eyeballs, mistaking them for lint. The forearms she takes wooden clothes pins to & hangs them from the aluminum awning just like her mother used to. Then the chest. The torso. The toes. They twitch —maybe to say hello, maybe help—communication these days, it's hard to say. Your mother's iPhone notifies her that a private plane nosedived into some fog. Her Bluetooth earpiece picks up that goats are doing yoga on her coworkers. Somewhere a Geiger counter oscillates between *we got this & oh my god.* Here, a spring breeze ruffles a bed of Easter lilies, billowing the bloated abdominal skin hanging over the porch swing. Your mother smiles —the backyard has never smelled so fresh.

Neighbors host a luau as barbeque and tiki torches
　　tinge the air,
and loneliness is the aftermath of a wildfire.

Near the highway, homeless men stake tents
　　on abandoned trails.
What's the difference between *free* and *pariah?*

A hobo squeegees idling cars. Their rapid strokes
　　scrub off mosquitoes
before green lights to efface past misfortunes.

Jimmy crushes blackberries in a bowl only for juices
　　to stain his T-shirt.
His mother bakes pie crust.

Crust. Crust. Why has the rain ceased?
Geologists lecture: a flood once excavated networks
　　of roots.

Waste land—where roots can't clutch crumbling red rock.
Here shrubs and weeds sprout along torrid banks
　　like fragments.

Grey is the New Grey

The sky is the shade of the asphalt. The sports car. The suit. It's gelid enough for the exhaust to be grey. The salesman's skin like a mummy—grey. The salmon tastes of lead. Which is the same as grey says the CDC, though they are unavailable to comment on the source. Would you dance in a caustic rain? a focus group asks as a camera zooms in on a smoking rose petal. You put your smart phone down & order the silverware, thinking counting carbs can be such a drag. After being stitched back together, your hair, in a certain light, looks platinum; luckily, it's all the rage to appear sage. So these are your options, the salesman says. You smile, chew your fork, capriciously sign some box. Two jars are retrieved from a satchel, then placed on the tablecloth; one labeled W, the other B. A flat screen in the corner cycles through headlines, the subtitles unable to keep pace. You unscrew both jars (How they reek of soggy newspaper!), then smear the white on one cheek, the black on the other. Your check, a waiter says.

& there's a rub. The cashier went on a smoke break & nobody has seen them since. There are twenty people in line, their cheeks desiccating into peach pits. Who will cover the tab? & who will allow it? & who bought stock in skin care? & who knows what's trending in health? & who should be sacrificed for beauty? & who saw the salesman drive home? He staggers inside, then stares at the walls of his guest room. For hours. Eventually hacking up some phlegm, he decides to paint the sheetrock. & as the brush swipes up, the town is rolled with fog.

iii

William Wordsworth's early lines were inspired
    by nature's spring.
His walks sparked a visionary gleam.

Highway marquee flashes: "Warning. Danger Ahead."
    Commuters daydream.
Patrolmen run radars in silence as wildflowers choke on heat.

Ultraviolet light triggers rapid melanin production
    in lifeguards.
Ogling adolescents splash to impress.

Years ago, father slept with bartenders, poured shots
    into our family tree.
His son OD'ed on exhaust. We cremated flesh. Spread ashes
    by the creek.

A counselor tells Jimmy to "branch out and relate
    with something."
Under the sun, a tributary traps Wild Turkey
    and Grey Goose bottles.

Where are the songs of spring?
I inhale tobacco, diesel and rubber burnt. Will these,
    my songs of summer be?

Fine Dining after a Draught from Rip's Flagon

The waiter asks, how would you like your
roadkill? without ever listing the night's
silverware special or a wine to be paired.
Speaking of wine, what had been in that flagon,
or those W & B jars—wait, across the aisle,
skewered to a spit,
is a squished squirrel with a putrid aroma
that keeps you from solving why
no one finds devouring rodents strange
or why the waiter's hair looks brittle
as if they too had been peeled from a tire;
tonight, you had expected seared Wagyu
or ideally escargot tongs, but this—
While the waiter waits for a reply,
you study the candle-lit shadows defining
their jaw line & briefly wonder if you could
sink your canines into their mesh, or
embrace a new aphrodisiac; however,
a whiff from your neighbor's squirrel,
drains color from your cheeks, & though
sunken, they tighten more, like a
salted-hide. That's all we have,
they say nonchalantly as if reading your
skepticism, as if the others surrounding you,
crowding, slipping knives into carcasses
was natural. Maybe you had never
eaten Wagyu, maybe species had gone extinct.

Fresh, you finally order, hoping
to avoid maggots or anything that might
weaken your stomach. Then the chef,
with a rusted Pontiac, drives the aisle &
lets opossum fall from their grill. It
still has dimension, a twitch. & from
the kitchen, while you chew, an
armadillo shell cracks & men
cough, or wheeze, as your hair bristles.

iv

When ancient Rome underwent droughts, men
    gave sacrifice, *aquilicium*, to Jupiter.
His wife, Juno, goddess of fertility, gives us June.

A wildfire sparks in a hay field. Stringers check
    camera batteries and GPS.
Bordering subdivisions load up trucks and pray.

Mother offered thanks and a mistake to the Clinic.
Mushrooms feast on decaying figs. In bourbon
    she found her comfort.

By the creek, Jimmy parks his Firebird, discovers
    doe tracks, and wonders
when solitude slips from peaceful into oppressive.

A priest's jubilation stems from an increase in attendance.
The congregation, bent over as one, whispers,
    "we'd settle for a hurricane."

Jupiter's red spot consists of cyclones
    churning eternally.
Our land stops storms.

A Bed of Bees

You read your fortune cookie:
April brings showers sweet with fruit
that end those droughts of March,
then asked to go by April. Later we
stood by a creek, when it was calm,
& saw a skyline upside down.
A passing plane wrote: April will be
the cruelest month. I wondered if you
did a downward dog, near the bank,
if you'd see the clouds or a plume
of smoke? I breathed into my fist
to keep myself warm; something
compelled my fingers to unfurl,
& there was a stamen in my palm.
You asked, which came first: the flower
or the bee? & I said, why should they matter
when neither of us take honey with our brie?
Off a bit, funnel clouds stretched like a claw
in a crane game, picking up a subdivision;
we were glad there was room for a high-rise now.
But then you trembled when I extended my hand.
I swear it's not radioactive;
WebMD has no idea why it's black,
crumbling. Something brushes your eyelash,
& there's a spasm in your eyes as you
text away. Were there bluebonnets by the creek,
last year? My memories are molting; my Sperry's
are crunching on a bed of bees. Even as I ask
April's doing cartwheels through a forest
fire, & the ash is doing cartwheels
off her flats, & I swear there's splendor

V

Miss Lonelyhearts writes his column for the depressed
    and decrepit.
When passing a mottled park, he prays for tears
    to water the ground.

Dragonflies crisscross over fire ants and cigarettes.
Wind carries smoke south. Will that burnt pine smell
    wake the lethargic?

Amusement park attendance declines. Bottled water
    prices increase
as children and elderly collapse in heat.

An unemployed man whines over a burnt house.
    Cameras zoom in.
Wildfire's carbon dioxide, combined with moisture,
    forms carbonic acid.

Jimmy follows the doe tracks to creek bed puddles.
Under plastic bags and algae, a branch protrudes
    from a biker's spine.

From its embalmed ashes, the phoenix resurrects.
I lay by the bank and lament a passing.

It's Fine

When *playing fifty-two* pick up
the four suits are: Denial, Anger, Bargain, De-

pression. A Roomba automatically cleans
the afternoon's ash. Bills are drafted monthly like clock

work. For the last two hours
I've been part of an online bidding war

for white noise. My closet is already full
with a year's supply. Playing

might not be the most apt word. Strug-
gle snags on the tongue though.

A ceiling fan flurries three suits out a high-rise window,
not before a charcuterie board shattered against a wall.

The sun rose twice before anyone realized honey
dripping from the ceiling. Fifty-two

seems too minute, but *thousands* comes too close.
It's fine, I say, which I often say

because I have always been attracted
to that pronoun. The distance *it*

allows, severing the link between what is heard
& what is meant. It'll be—

fine. Still my glasses fog when
I hyperventilate. In Key West,

the roosters crow at all hours of the day.
Do they not want to admit that sunrise came,

& they missed it? Or did somebody suck
the sun through a straw, & they crow,

hoping not to let on their vision has been compromised?

vi

While clouds and smoke blend, a couple sips hurricanes.
A woman shrieks when a bird snatches her garnish.

Puritans feigned a devil in the woods.
What must have Moses thought when the bush self-combusted?

Firefighters chase flare ups, unequipped to guess their births.
The news showcases eye-witness testimonies and before and
after photos.

Jimmy pulls the biker out of the muck and weeps.
My brother was Jimmy. The creek and deceased
    consume our tears.

Each evening the retired water flower pots, only to
    watch them wilt.
In their age is the knowledge they'll sprout anew.

O creek, what sacrifice have we neglected to pay?
Under the sun, commuters burn up interstate and fuel my call.

Call Me Bonzo

God keep me from ever completing anything
Melville

I'm obsessed
with history's collection of fragments.

The waiter with the shorthand
juggling ten tables. The

Tinder profiler,
who smudges their height, income & fetishes.

For small erections
may be finished by their first architects;

Never mind the geneticist's attempt to manipulate
adenine, cytosine, guanine, & that T base, or

the disciples of Turing, the mapping
of Xanadu in *Kubla Khan.*

grand ones, true ones,
ever leave the copestone to posterity.

How our own per-
sonal histories intertwine with the larger—

God keep me

from ever completing

During a rehearsal, Bonham took
forty shots of vodka to the liver; the weight

of his imagined inadequacies held
the vomit in his lungs, as well

as every Zeppelin song bottled
or dissipated inside Plant   the fans

This whole book is but a   —*nay,*
but   *of a draught.*

But what if like Galahad
        had already reached

perfect   ? Or what if
picked off the vine before sour

no. Why do some   commit
suicide for organs to form during

embryonic   develop   ? Why
            DNA hardwired   gametes   com-

bine? Is   power
incomplete? Should we

why   necessary
survive   pilgrimages

Oh, T , Strength,
C   , Pati

IV

LETTERS TO SOMEWHERE

I promised you a love letter, and got as far as:
Dear Dad,

I left lots of white space, hoping
                    you'd either fill in what you knew I
or what I should
              Truthfully,
                        my counselor's idea
  for getting closer to

I leave the letter in a drawer of a coffee table,
        and go about my day.

Rosie keeps looking to me for answers, but—

she won't let me secure the windows. Would she let me dig a
foxhole? Like the one you stood in the night I was born. Next to
your commanding officer, cigar between your fingers, saying:
doc says he'll be   a few more weeks. Like weathermen,
doctors first predictions are seldom
right. Do you think

        you felt guilty for driving from D.C. to the hospital

    I was leaving
                  hospital for home,
                     and as a baby
                          sensed the distance?
          Or was distance created
                 you worked nights
                       I slept, and when I studied

you slept? It's like

               timelines never synced.

A police officer in the checkout line of the supermarket said: stay indoors. And they should be right. Right? You were an officer and never lied. Right?

I put this in the coffee table too and go about my day.

Dear Dad,
I—

Rosie keeps asking why strangers are limping down the
sidewalk. If they can, why can't we? And I tell her:

which never satisfies her. I must admit it never satisfies me
either. But why would she want to limp like that? I can tell you,
Rumple shots aren't igniting that stagger. There's a Cub Scout
manual in the coffee table, which tells how to tie knots, and start
a fire, but there's no mention of how to build a bridge, or fill
white space, or fix a radio, or reassure—

Did you and I ever go on that camping trip?

I went to grab a sheet of paper from inside the coffee table and found this:

O Evie,

 I'm so sorry I shut you out. When you asked to hula hoop, I just wanted to run laps around the block, & when you asked how to plant forget-me-nots, I couldn't risk the flowers not surviving the summer. You must've thought me such the bitch, but I had a secret to keep. A secret nobody knew I had. That's why when you asked if I'd help plan our parent's thirtieth anniversary, I cried.

 Evie, I'm beginning to think we'll never leave this living room.

 If nobody talks about it, did it happen? I ask myself that more & more.

I wish you could answer me,

Sis

On the other side is a naked picture of two people, just waving. There are a few others, but I can't bring myself to read them.

Dear Dad,
I lo—
I lost track of how many strangers are Evie. Every Jane Doe
with a limp is Evie. It's a wonder the glass hasn't shattered from
Rosie's screams. She won't stay much longer. I hear it in her
pacing. But how else to keep us safe? She asked this morning if I
remember the day we met?

Origin stories shut me down. Which is something I should've
said. Or did I say? My counselor
said I need

        work on   , on asking for

                        Did I ever

tell you I

        Did I ever

             your birthday calls?

   How it hurt

         you joke about the

              the foxhole,

    like laughter

        force a play
from history or tragedy into a comedy?

Evelyn,
Evie,
Sis,

Somebody is sleeping by the curb. They haven't moved in three days. I say sleeping because no vultures have swooped in to sniff their vitals. I'd check but the authorities said: stay indoors. Strange, but as I write this, I realize we never mingled with anyone on this street—can't even say if they're a neighbor or vagrant. What would you do? Would you help—

Rosie hasn't left the bed in a week, so she's not aware yet. Would this be the time to board the windows? Crepe myrtle bark and empty water bottles have partially covered their head. Internet searches returned goats doing yoga, then *connection lost*. If only Rosie and I remembered how to connect with each other. Or with the outside. Or with—

Dear Dad,

I loved riding shotgun and giggling with a CB radio while you drove around the block, sirens flashing. Your mission to get me sleeping. Do you think—

Should we have shifted the squad car into reverse until the GPS said: starting route.

V

UNNATURAL SLEEP

Canvas of the Big Bang

There is an art exhibit in a downtown loft. A journalist says, this shows potential, as she steps across the museum rope. Brain & bone fragments are splattered against a living room wall. It's a little mainstream, the coroner says. The artist stands by his recliner, a pistol by his sneakers. Would you mind discussing your work? the journalist asks. The artist moves his lips, though his tongue is sprinkled amongst the frontal lobe. I was searching for answers, he mouths, & then look. As if on cue, the city shuts off the loft's electricity. No one knows if this is for dramatic flare or an unpaid bill, but they continue to watch his mouth, molars rolling out the back of his head like casings. Not sure he answered your question, the coroner says. Well he has no brain, the journalist says. But then moonlight weaves through the blinds, through the artist's mouth, splashing onto the canvas, glistening off the bone fragments. Sort of looks like the Milky Way, the journalist says. Maybe that's how the Big Bang happened, the coroner says. Lamps on the end tables sense where this line of reasoning will lead & jump from the window sill. By god, the journalist says as they both genuflect, skepticism transmuting into spirituality. The air conditioner now worries that humidity will compromise its universe. The moon lingers, for a second, for eternity, while the artist's mandible flounders against the carpet.

Minute Maid Cadence

Welcome, the attendant waves
after hiking the price on the A-frame stand.

On the corner of Congress & Crawford, a man
bangs on five gallon buckets & trash can lids,

which partially drowns out you & I
running over our plan for being caught on camera.

One, Two, Three, Four—Cue
the setting sun on a closed retractable roof,

because few can handle the Houston heat
& even fewer the spotlight. On the curb

of Minute Maid, this tycoon flaunts his commemorative
brick to prospective clients, then secretly

pops an upper because it's up, up, up to the suite
life—& what's he then that says we play

the villain—Security, well, has the gates blocked,
because rumors circulate of a player that tapped

their cleats into the red clay at home plate
& up oozed this black gold. What is

the key to prominence? Now,
a helicopter's spotlight & the moon compete

for the best angle, while journalists, scouts
& prospectors research historic springs:

the Fountain, Spindletop, Springer Dinger,
& this thick tar rises from home plate, disente-

grating into a black mist that's hazardous to inhale,
& on the curb, outside the stadium, you flail a soiled

handkerchief & sing: "I stole, I stole their key,
publish me!" & then I pull out my handkerchief,

so we may wave to one another.

What do we say to the god of death?

Everyone hates an ending wrapped too neatly
or that asks more questions than it answers

or rushes to the credits after a well-paced story
like *Game of Thrones;*
                where's the build
                      up to Euron's arrow
                 piercing a dragon
       not once (but twice!)
                 how are we to feel the gravity
of losing a child;
            if Tyrion committed treason
                     why
      was there no death by fire
   only Jesus
            enters a cave a dead man,
then is reborn the hand of God;
            why do you stand
      to pee during this scene;
if Jamie sleeps
            with Brienne then
  why rush off to Cersei in the same episode?
      You whisper
           you can relate.
There's such a gulf
                    generated by post-binge
                  depression
     like when I stand in the driveway
        after we cram a week's affair into an hour
         then watch you drive   *to him.*

Can't speak ill
                    of the Mad Queen
            as you know, the Joker says, madness is

like gravity   all it takes is a little push;
                ash drizzles all through the subdivision;
                    you spew stomach acid
                            afraid to ask who's
            the father;
                    millions sign a petition
        for what?
                        If Schrödinger's box
held instead a script, finished or blank, the box would

tumble off a throne, the screen fading to black,
the audience only hearing the crackle of fire.

Risk Assessment

If you fuck in the shower to spice up your quarantine,
historical charts suggest your lotioned toes will slide off

the tub's ledge, his weakened biceps unable to lift
your thigh; failure, however, is a position

neither of you understands, so when you attempt
one more thrust, his foot will slip up, the faucet

bludgeoning his head, & you will think (a little too late),
most household accidents happen in the bathroom—

when wisps of vermillion blend with the crystalline-water,
then whisk toward the drain, how you assess the situation's

severity will be challenged. Maybe you'll beg
for advice, & an overworked tele-doc will say ennui

is a currency with no market or exchange rate; rest up,
which will be easy to obey, because his body won't budge

except for the hair, which twists in the current,
drawing his cells back into a primordial vortex,

swirling with his neighbor's buttery diarrhea, another's broken
condom, perhaps a child's shaken goldfish? Yes,

the sewer always seeks to control how we disintegrate
into digestible compounds, as if we should no longer seek

control, but there's a crack in the system,
his consciousness now evaporating into a gathering mist,

where not five miles from your apartment, you speed
toward an intersection, his bloating-body in the backseat,

droplets all around the car bursting: stop!
as perpendicular, a single man wearing two masks,

idles through the same intersection.

Confection Sprinkled with Love

The marquis flashes: 'Tis the season
of cold witch's tits; wrap up,

which triggers a panic attack: how much
salary is under the hypoallergenic tensile?

O hell! Best hide the high-end utensils,
'cus that distant relative gonna cut you

off, like a honking horn cuts Jingle Bells
when you merge into the mall's parking lot.

Empty shelves, empty promises, empty—
omg is that a limited-edition? A

stranger's hand reaches out
(Mariah Carey's All I Want for Christmas

blaring through every speaker), O
germs! But do they want to carol Joy

to the World? Nah, they just want
to punch you in the face. Packing

peanuts rain from the rafters, black mist
blows thick, addling their brains. Ain't that

the shit. Everyone films, or everyone joins
in the brawl. Ticker-tape receipts, unbridled

frustrations are unpacked from deep, deep
pockets, then blood—but who's to say it's

blood? No, deep pockets, ~~then blood,~~ empty
for confection sprinkled with love.

A friendly summertime

warning: if you or I run when the heat index exceeds
one hundred, those blaring AC

from parked cars will live stream:
commentary: livin' their best life

OR must have a death wish.
In the frame's edge, a squirrel will chase

anonymity up & down a maple tree.
Leaves, desiccated & flighty,

will chip off as if at cross purposes
& though blurry, draw the viewer's eye.

NOW, somewhere off screen will be
sheets of algae, Styrofoam spit cups, upturned

minnows, our new sneakers pounding,
pounding—partially repaired

myocardium tearing, repairing, no
tearing, desiring to re-

capture the str-
ength to test

limits.

A Red Pill

In this film, you & I marveled
at Keanu's ability to stop a bullet;

a new age Superman, relearning
the boundaries of his world;

not unlike, the man who peddled
Roman candles to us, despite an unpre-

cedented drought banning fireworks.
Years later, when the thrill of CGI

fades, we choke on Hugo's classification
of us as virus; we do more than

consume & multiple. Someday
if virulent weather pins us

into bunkers, will we think
back on Keanu as he opens his eyes

for the first time, choking up
amniotic fluid, plugs all down

his arms & spine & wonder
how we too can wake up?

The Art of Going Green

Don't ask us what's in a name; we've
set fire to the rose bushes, condemned the balcony,

even sprinkled pesticide inside the aside.
Don't ask us about the art of going green; we've

buried our kin in unmarked graves for the blow flies
to breed. "Bonzo" (aka Mr. Deaton) looks semi-green

after that line. Revision: We return to the earth.
This seems less genuine, however, for what do we

return? Mr. Deaton, with his pining, is less *on*
these days, so in secret we call him Mr. Deat.

Don't look now, but a green-eyed monster bursts our
ear drums on a piccolo. The Hulk, laughing, slaps

the melody & the monster's hand across
state lines. Question: did exposure to gamma rays

or ultra-violent rays turn the skin green? Behind
a pulpit, the priest, with a voice full of money,

says something inspirational, but the mic cuts off.
A one-handed Mr. Deat pirouettes in agony. Baby

It's Cold Outside is canceled on the airwaves,
similarly, the south is shutdown by an ice storm.

The two are unrelated, we're sure. *Global
warming* abdicates to *climate change*. What's in

a name? We sneak a silent *h* onto Mr. Deat's,
snickering at our esoteric play. We also stock supplies

for hurricane parties—oversized candles, generators,
kegerators, punch bowls, ganja bowls; we'll

welcome 500 year floods, maybe 800 as long
as there's no 6000. We take selfies

with sparking transformers for the backdrop. Waters rise,
then recede, or at least we're sure they will

recede as mattresses drift down driveways toward
something undeniable. No sweets, no sorrows,

just partings. Oh & a calling card—sewage creeping
up the sheetrock. Maybe the mold will be natural?

Mr. Deat-*h* naturally says little, so we fill, & we kill
uncomfortable silences with fresher & stranger natures.

The Forever Spring Break

Our physics professor taught us that a body in motion,
deteriorates in motion, then said, see you in a week.

It's past a week, & all we've seen are grooves
in the carpet from our pacing, & hair that weaves

into the shower drain. We test new hobbies,
& we pick up forgotten projects from the shelf.

We nightly scour the light pollution for omens,
& wonder if "the evil eye of the sky" is Halley's comet,

or Big Brother. Anti-comet pills & gas masks
remain in the attic. Still, we tune the television

to channel 18, & though it airs only static,
we believe it will show the True Way,

or traffic routes to the shoreline. The neighbor's
cat keels over, unexpectedly, & we try

to research taxidermy techniques, but the computer
crashes as well—a latent Y2K response,

or domestic subterfuge? How we teeter between waiting
it out & building angst. Like in our backyard,

buried beneath an unkempt compost heap,
are blueprints for a Hadron Collider. If we connect

K'NEKs, should we construct an accelerator? A black hole
is in our molar, which the dentist won't drill

till travel restrictions lift. We currently avoid
the calendar on the fridge—fake news claims the

Mayan calendar ran out of pages. We feel this holiday
runs short on squares. Do we continue to

craft distractions or risk introspection?

Pneumonoultramicroscopicsilicovolcanoconiosis

A factitious word from a puzzle league in '35,
never mind that it would bleed over a Scrabble

board, like bourbon down the drain in AA.
P45 is a syzygy of morphemes,

a synonym for silicosis, like *game*
is equivalent to *frolic*, *prank*, *quarry*,

schema, *sudden death*. When we think of
a volcano's invisible breath, swirling inside

the lungs, we picture Black Sunday,
a behemoth of uprooted sod that serrated

& swallowed the south. Sometimes we tire
of word play, & play Deal or New Deal.

Twenty-six cases range from stimulus checks
to Social Security, & are held by models

wearing masks; for verisimilitude, we
alternate between being contestants

& being bankers, a Hoover Dam
between us. So when we pick cases

& when we gamble, we can righteously
laugh at playing reality's game. When

all's exhausted, I'm compelled to close Words
with Friends, then you open Safari, refresh

the page to view a new body count.

Stocking up on the Essentials

Will we grow to eat the
disinfectant wipes & toilet paper

because the pantry holds
a surplus of their

off brands? One ply folded
over may make a sandwich, but so no one faces

starvation, will some still have to
scavenge for roadkill if the

armadillo can be scraped from the floor?
& will we sip bleach, &

(pinky's out), will we recite every
mandate that extends our day

by one? If the
visions & revisions of the paper

give us pause, like a good little boy
should we quickly transition? Will what brings

us peace is praying the essential question pile is no more?

Playing for the Ruins

Pink Floyd's *Live at Pompeii*, 1972

The heart of the sun erupted
from a raging volcano, christening

an amphitheater in pumice.
A wall of speakers reverberates

off cracked stone & weeds. A gong
eclipses the sun & the moss's applause.

An echo of a distant time
oozes through our television screen, comes

reminding us of a fall before the Roman Fall.
Our computer streams Facebook live, the

local musician crooning into his computer, the
hanged paintings holding their clap, the

stillness lingering like the fevers
of those hosed to ventilators.

Death, Contagion & Unnatural Sleep

When Shakespeare says someone dies,
he sometimes means they orgasm,

& if we're honest, we do the same when semen
stains our sheets, & we tally whose pull out game

will be the strongest. Other games we play
include how deep can we shove a testing swab up our holes,

can we tickle a neuron, or how much bleach
can we coat the asparagus with, how much can we cheers,

because there are fifty shades of climaxing,
& we must explore everyone.

When Byron has Manfred say, "Old Man! 'Tis not so difficult
to die," we battle this assumption with polyps in our lungs:

sometimes whiskey impedes our performance
& sometimes the lassitude of being on 24/7 downs our desire

& if we're honest, blue light enervates our eyes,
our lives, but smart phone fatigue does not mean we lie

on tufts of weeds, waiting to expire,
because we are young men, young women with the longevity of
vampires,

& even if the world ends with a whimper,
we linger, & we linger, & we linger.

When Tyler Durden says he has insomnia,
like toddlers we too fight against the night & we

Gee Brain, what are we gonna do tonight?

Cartoon villains once desired world dominance,
but bad luck or bad monologues would foil

their attempts to stay on top. Now, real villainy
is hitting the pillow, then instantly hearing Tears

for Fears play, "Everybody Wants to Rule the World,"
through a mallet-smashed alarm clock. Lately, when we sleep,

Plague carrying rats scamper across our eyelids.
Narf! Who would want the pressure of responding

to eight billion emails? Tectonic plates shifted
to socially distance Pangea, only for the internet

to rope them back together. Who would want
to rule the world? When we wake, our browser

is stuck on yesterday's article. A bad monologue:
maybe a virus broke the computer,

maybe rats zapped by a shrink ray snuck
into the motherboard & are gnawing

on the circuits, maybe our mother left
a Post-It on the fridge, saying: sanitize

the produce, & our laptop is tired of us ignoring
the message, maybe the bully at the bus stop,

who terrorized us in the third grade, cussing
& punching their way to the top, finally learned

how to reach through the internet, maybe a virus
broke the internet. We live in snow globes

of anxiety. Gee brain, what are we gonna do
tonight? A billion neurons fire: close the eyelids,

but when muscles translate the signal, a pinky
flicks the globe off a shelf.

The Art of Going Extinct

Don't question us on the intricacies of Rapture;
we're captured by the five extinctions already on the books,

captivated by Lady Lazarus & the three of her nine lives,
but we're not yet capitulated. Don't

ask us for Seconds; we're still flummoxed
that algae's nascent zapped all the O2 from the ocean,

still freaked that seaweed hardens our double
scooped ice cream, & still fixated on the fast-winding hand

of the Doomsday clock. Yes, we vacation at Yellowstone,
genuflect to the geyser, pray to the super

volcano—acknowledging the ash from two past,
that told the world it's time to slumber. Don DeLillo's

White Noise asks us: can we make a refrigerator? Can
we explain a radio? Tell the Middle Ages how to

stop an epidemic raging? We dump our
HelloFresh into the trash bin, then step into

a Golden Corral's lunch buffet. A five-year old
shakes their toy T-Rex, then slams them

into the tabletop. From the buffet, we
seek Yangtze Sturgeon, Pinta Giant Tortoise,

Dodo rolls, & the server says,
they're currently out of stock.

Some feign outrage, some
dip their fingers into soy sauce,

gnaw on their cuticles,
& you bow to those

that have gone
before us.

A Case for Icarus

Icarus is often portrayed as flying too close to the sun,
or given wax wings that melt from the sun,

or given explicit instructions to stay away from the sun,
or told not to fly too low,

given the sea could disintegrate the wings,
or that Daedalus built the wings to help

him escape a tower, or that they were imprisoned
in a tower to protect the secret of the labyrinth.

* * *

In elementary school, our class went on a field trip designed to
teach us how to team-build or appreciate the sun. At the end, we
had to climb a thirty-foot totem pole & leap for a golden ring. To
this day, I'm unsure if a fear of heights or falling had me climb
up the pole, then climb down.

Williams & Auden focused on a painting, not the myth. The
painting focused on the crowd, not the myth. On the splash, not
the fall. If they had autopsied the wings, would they have
spotted sun-scorched wax?

Rayman, my favorite video game character, had no neck, no arms, no legs, but still (head floating), managed to move his sneakers in sync with the directional pad. Rayman also had a knack for throwing his disembodied hand toward golden rings, enabling him to hop islands or ascend the clouds.

In 1862, Glaisher & Coxwell ascended in a hot air balloon. Their instruments read atmospheric pressure all the way up to 37,000 feet. The hope was to better understand weather patterns. One must have said to the other: fuck, it's cold.

The Day After Tomorrow, though a flawed film, had an interesting theory on Earth's endgame: climate change would not lead to melted butter but to those crystals meat collects when left too long in the freezer.

In the living room, I played Rayman while my mom got the call her mom had passed. She told us Grams was in a better place as Rayman landed between islands, then respawned.

But would Icarus' wings have melted like the Greeks taught? What did they know of heaven? The atmosphere? Of hubris? If frozen, would his wings fissure under a forceful flap? Would they shatter if flicked by a jealous god?

On average, fingernails grow 3.47 mm a month, hair 12.7 mm.
On average, California slips 35 mm a year, while the sea rises
3.4 mm. On average, the human conscience expands _____ a
generation.

To this day, I'm unsure of the headstone's inscription, the
scripture, the dress my mom picked, the melody looped as we
filled the church. I remember the viewing, some flicking tissues,
others slapping pews, my cousins & I gathered with our backs
toward the casket, playing Hearts.

Cellular senescence is the result of telomere shortening,
prohibiting cells from dividing, thus leading to aging.

* * *

Grief is a labyrinth some choose not to enter,
or utterly lose themselves inside,

twisting & festering memories into a maddening guilt,
or brush away as something natural,

or naturally market for those seeking self-help,
or being self-reliant inspires them to build wings,

which on this day seems prudent as an ocean rises
& icicles collect on the ceiling.

When Hamlet has Insomnia

Everything is a copy of a copy of a copy
Chuck Palahniuk

i

When we die will there be dreams; after all,
we've slipped off our memory-foam mattress.

Makes us wonder, perhaps admire,
those that toil to postpone it,

but I mean who'd bear their lashes for wrinkles,
the boss's lectures, the stranger's sneers,

the sludge of unrequited love, the backward laws,
the impotence of presidents, & the disdain

for anyone that can easily checkout.

ii

If our cellphones pass through a dead zone,
will we still be connected?

Gives us anxiety just to think
that time existed before the internet,

because who'd plan their weekend by carrier pigeon,
the missionary's word, the town crier's rant,

the eldest child's shortfalls, the no mail Sundays,
the nerve of Puritans, & the audacity

of anyone living off the grid.

iii

Let's say Opening Day passes, & there's no baseball
will our lives be reruns & infomercials?

Trapped in stasis, we marvel at the non-sports fan
who fills hours of a day doing—well we don't know;

surely no one could work 9 to 5 then bring their work home,
or scan the news, or read the bombastic blogs,

or watch the Bachelor, the unscheduled sequel,
or abide by the HOA, or despise

cheering for talent & perseverance.

iv

What if Mr. Deat-*h* doesn't approve these questions,
& drags our voice to the recycle icon?

Fuels are insomnia,
wondering if people sleep easily—

seriously ~~who survives the void between Facebook likes,~~
~~or the fact-checker's jail, or the Messenger duels,~~

~~or being blocked across platforms, the edited posts,~~
~~or the admin's approval, or fury~~

~~for having to~~ praise Mr. Deat-*h*^ON.

v

O god what if drug stores won't restock sleeping pills,
& our minds forget this progression of questions,

& the risk of heart disease, diabetes, dissociation,
& we become no different than zombies, our

bodies tearing between wanting to fall apart, &
answering a higher call ▮▮▮▮ O god

what if we're never allowed to sleep, &
our minds forget what we had for lunch, & we

bite more than we can chew?

vi

Estimated Time of Arrival

We lollygag in the ~~loft's~~ Apocalypse's lobby. There is something appetizing about the room: a chandelier of locust, a bubbling, red koi pond, scabs on the sofas. Do we desire an end? Perhaps, who cancels their cable provider before a series finale? Who wants Calomel for their melancholy? a vendor yells from the Apocalypse's patio; Mercury will get you closer to god or to good health. We shuffle outside, the patio a series of concentric decks, shrouded in mist. Do we descend the cobblestone steps or return to the lobby? Another vendor raises a bottle from a lower deck: RadiThor, for those suffering from FOMO, is "a cure for the living dead," guaranteed "perpetual sunshine." Curious, we thumb a brochure: radium water, engineered to provide energy (potentially cure impotence), may fracture bones or cloud eyes. We ready Apple pay, but then close the app. How would we reach our destination? Tape our eyelids open to breathe the sunshine? On the bottom deck, we don our souvenir T-shirts that read, We Survived. With Vin Mariani in hand, we reach a beach (the mist finally rising), toast to Dionysius, then to cocaine—to hell if we miss Charon's cruise ship. Waves crest & glyphs appear in the froth; maybe it's a message for us, but our translator is further down the shore, haggling with a local over hydroxychloroquine, coughing. A rotting whale carcass invites us inside, but we'll linger here a little longer, then linger some more.

VI

SOMEWHERE

V

Trauma Counselor

How many times must she say they are not PEZ dispensers? The counselor's not sure. Her upper-half gyrates as her toes, bent inward, still relearn to walk (yoga pants luckily stretch with her gait). Now, just because someone ran past them one time & said, Argh, don't bite me, does not mean they had to adopt the identity of a novelty item. She stands behind the cash register, while they collect between the aisles. & yet during meetings, someone will always grab their scalp, whether their neck's been sliced by a broken wine bottle, or blown to hell by some high-powered rifle, pull it back & ask if anyone would like to try their tongue.

Mind you, they're not asking in their native tongue, so that's half the problem. After they reawakened (or whatever you want to call it) only impressions of their past lives remained. New languages formed. New identities. Someone once thought this extra sight made them a surveillance camera. Their head swiveled 360 degrees every conversation (some ligaments must've deteriorated before the reawakening). Do you remember how it happened? she asked. Those tapes have been scrubbed, they replied. Do you know where you are? she asked. That's a blind spot, they said. Do you remember if you had children? she asked. Their head sporadically swiveled, their vertebrae clicking.

The counselor can't say she's exhausted (with so much time away from her body, she's more or less forgotten what's attached to that emotion), but it's taxing leading this support group. Her knees still struggle to bend as her legs drag her outside this convenience store, just for some peace. There's beauty in the splintered powerlines, the graffiti, the vines sprouting through the parking lot. The scattered limbs in varying stages of decomp are pleasant reminders of what she used to be, or could have been. Not that she feels the warmth (due to nerve damage), but the sun even blossoms today.

No one has bothered to repair the city, so maybe that's why some linger. She says some, because the group is always in flux. The counselor's well aware that memories have atrophied, much like the months or years they've been in this state, but faces have a way of sticking. Why only yesterday someone staggered through those sliding glass doors, missing part of their scalp & entire left arm. During group, they gabbed about having to helplessly watch their pristine figure languish. How did they remember? Anyone else would have referred to themselves as a cash register, money always being withdrawn or inserted, but this guy painted fragments of their previous life..

A deer with half an antler trollops between turned over shopping carts. A deer or a goat? The counselor wishes she had a fraction of that man's memory—had she been essential, did she have a sister, is she sprinting this way, but all that stuck was tossing some antique wood paneling after a flood. If there was more, then she'd know if they all gravitated toward each other or the convenience store. If she got elected or stuck with this group. & why all members confuse themselves for machines. Maybe being ripped from their bodies so inexplicably shattered their psyches. Maybe having started with questionable character, they reverted to ones and zeros. Or maybe with their humanity so altered, technology is all they could recognize.

& it's not just memories. The counselor loses sizeable chunks of time, especially in the evening. As if when she's not engaging, she's a laptop in hibernation, which is ludicrous, she knows. Much like these shadows she swears wave at her.

Her toes straighten slightly as she works her way back inside. If the sun won't break her down, then she might as well lead. There's this new one that's convinced he's a cellphone. How are you operating without electricity? she asks, trying to draw attention to the absurdity of the belief. We're sorry, they say, but the number you're trying to reach is disconnected; please hang up & try again. Denial is always so crafty. Do you have a SIM card? she asks; can the police track you? Now playing a track by The Police, they say. She lets the session shift to static, because they can't remember the lyrics, not even the melody.

IV

Backseat Driver

He told himself not to bite Jeff's neck. Not that he had any control, but he told himself. & then Bill walked into the room, & asked why Jeff had left the printer jammed. Bill probably wished he had stayed in his office, because both men mauled him. Then nobody in the office got work done that day.

He hovers somewhere inside the brain's synapses, fully aware of the moment, but unable to control his body. The wind rolls a tube of lipstick, kicked from a purse. It's sad to watch himself devolve. He used to hit the gym six days a week. Had a solid physique. Well, decent at least. Now he barely keeps skin on his bones. Walks with that obnoxious gait. The only time he runs is when someone shrills, but with so few left in this subdivision, he rarely chases anyone.

His body trips over a curb & into a crepe myrtle. Pigeons stare from their powerlines. He's tried suggesting he eat better. He's even tried picking up sirloins at HEB, but his knuckles scraped right over them. If only his body did more than bite the people, he might keep on a little weight.

He used to blame Lana for this. One morning, maybe a month ago, she kept eyeballing his donut, as her mouth frothed, & her eyes kind of glazed, but it turns out she just wanted his hand. & well, that was it. If Lana & him could talk now, he's sure they would patch things. After all—the body that bit him was no more Lana, than the body that bit Jeff was him. But he's not sure if Jeff would feel the same way. Or Jesus, Bill.

Mustangs & Jaguars are pinned against light poles, some tattooed with red handprints. Trashcans & recycling bins litter the street, spin aside as his body limps toward an intersection. Once he strained so hard to exert his will, that he popped into another's head. This store owner, crunched up behind some trash bags, was sleeping in a sewer drain. His body, dragging its feet, passed over the poor bloke, then bam! they both sunk into one of those Virgin Islands. A pleasant enough dream, but the store owner must have thought he was there to bite him, because he had a heart attack.

He's tried to repeat this anomaly, sink into other parts of his body, maybe even a dream, tell his body to do skull crushers with dumbbells instead of, you know, & help it reobtain some of his mojo, but the thing is is that it never sleeps. Never. Occasionally his body goes dormant, & he fishes around for a synaptic connection, but there's not much there. Not at all. His body loses more of his hair, which he feels partially guilty for, because his mother always said he'd bald prematurely. A car backfires, & his body starts that gait again. He just wishes—he wishes his body would listen.

But there it goes, dragging its feet into a convenience store. It helps when the doors are automated. If it hadn't been for automated doors, they'd still be trapped in the office. How undeniably frustrating to visualize the exit, then for days ping pong around the supply closet, ram into the bathroom mirrors, attack the electric hand dryers. The occasional thud of a nosediving blue jay was the only thing helping nudge him along.

Not sure why he staggered in here. The car has been against a stop sign for a month, an SUV trying to escape the office parking lot pinning it there. Oh the keys fell through his pocket days ago. He wishes it had a better pair of shoes. There's almost no skin on his soles anymore. & of course the attendant vacated shop weeks ago. So even if his body sought a protein shake, it couldn't order one here. Sometimes he swears it has no sense of direction. But how to guide something that won't listen?

The shelves are void of food. Condensation pools around the opened freezer doors. Though it's mildly intriguing that his body passed a row of Dr. Scholl's insoles & poorly stitched baseball caps, it's so dull just watching. It's a wonder they haven't been shot. Maybe people aren't allowed to carry anymore. Or maybe they all have rotten aim. Maybe someday he'll successfully project his will, ask for his body's input, even if monosyllabic grunts make for a horrid conversationalist.

Ants colonize around the cash register. Why is he still here? He asks himself that sometimes. Unfinished business? He was supposed to pick up some dry cleaning that evening after work, but he certainly won't need that suit anymore. Eventually he had planned on proposing to Penelope, but last he saw half her face was missing. Shotgun shell. Actually in a store much like this one. She must've finished everything before that shot, because she didn't linger. Not even for a second. Was it this store? Either way, he's—mostly sure he locked the front door before leaving for work, but for good measure let's see if his body will check: hey, you, hey

As he rambles, his body loses a finger, jammed by the automated doors. It's amazing the lack of common sense.

Still, he thought about setting up a blind date. You know, to atone for Penny, but it's so socially distant. It never mingles with its own kind. Just rushes toward those shrilling people.

& sure he's thought about abandoning it, but he only escaped its head with the sewer guy.

The sun is so resplendent, that he almost feels the warmth. Much like when Richard from accounting passed him yesterday. He felt like Richard asked him to bring kolaches to the staff meeting. Maybe he was in denial. & it's no surprise that he didn't recognize his body, chowing down on some lady in a wheelchair. If he hadn't seen his from day one, he wouldn't have recognized him either. & sure, *maybe* he could have steered him right, but it wasn't his place.

If Jeff crosses his path again, he'll just straight up tell him it was Lana's fault, somehow. He ought to believe that. Right?

Golden casings, sprinkled on the lawns, refract the sunlight. A toddler, missing one leg, slaps its palm against the pavement, pulling its body toward a storm drain. Organs are teepeed over a trailer bed. He's begun to forget some things. His name being the biggest one. But hopefully if he ends up somewhere, & there's a roll call, somebody will recognize him, & nudge him, & say, hey

man, that's you. He forgets why he worked in that office, or for
how long. He forgets how long he's been like this. He forgets the
favors he meant to cash in, or the blackmail he might've known.
He forgets—

Hey, was that his house?

Ugh, & there goes a whole arm. It walked straight into that
speeding Humvee. It never looks where it's going. Never. He
wishes it would take better care of itself. He really does. He used to
take such good care of himself.

III

American Dreamer

His baby. Nap can't imagine what they've done to her. Ransacked. Hell, simply ruined. & it's not like he didn't try to protect her. When that girl, with the sports bra & tank top, looked like she would shove her hand into the register. Buck shot. One of her fingers even clipped by the money drawer. All those dollars—simply ruined. & those uncivil screams. Must have been three more that tried to highjack the register. Where did they spring from? Normal customers are unruly, but respect boundaries. Seven days of beating these screamers back. It's his right to protect himself. His store, his baby. He's so sorry he had to abandon her.

The pandemonium of it all drove Nap underground. He sighs as he strokes his unloaded shotgun. Right now blood's pooling in the Slim Jim jar. Nobody will buy those. Waste. Such waste. & who knows what smells are seeping into the sheetrock. You can't scrub those out. Probably smells like this wretched sewer drain. He hopes it's not as sully. Rat droppings. Week old diapers. Talk about ripe. Just had to run out of shotgun shells. & those uncivil screamers never ceasing their onslaught for that register. Academy closed. Aggravating. & the police said vandals were a low priority. The first couple calls. Line was nothing but static later.

Nap needs to get back. No telling how many days have passed in this sewer; the screams fade in & out; sunlight rarely stretches through the storm drain or manhole. He needs to sweep all the shattered glass. The air conditioning bill will surely be out of control. & the expired Hawaiian rolls. The stolen twelve packs. Insurance won't cover any of that. Especially not the candy bars he nabbed. After all, there was no guarantee of another meal. Not that he'd steal from himself, but still—.

Who's there? he asks. All I've got are Paydays

Stupid—now they'll think he's a walking ATM.

& buck shot, he says.

That should deter even those uncivil screamers. But god, what if? A relative could adopt his baby. He thinks his brother is listed in the will. Not that he would squeegee the window panes once a week. Or rotate the Twinkies—

Thank god—it's just a dog. A drooling dog. Must be dehydrated. Is it smiling or snarling? Easy, now. Should've brought those bottled.

You're selling crawfish out of a white ice chest. Four dollars a pound. Winter lasted longer this season, so the mud bugs are small, mostly dead, which a guy in a baseball jersey hints at, trying to finagle the price to three a pound. You think to yourself you'll never afford that convenience store selling only skimpy, limp bugs, as you hoist three sacks into their truck bed. The truck sinks into the asphalt, which trucks do, you suppose.

You think, Don't I already own the convenience store? The crawfish was years ago, on a corner adjacent to the store. You'd stare & stare as a caravan of minivans pulled up, then pulled out. The symbiosis of it all. Your heart somewhere behind those glass doors..

You walk toward where it should be, & end up in a basement. There are soggy newspapers clumped against the molding, papier-mâché pictures, molding cardboard boxes. You don't remember holding a mop, but know the place needs cleaning, & there's no one else. A mosquito bites you. You don't know why this makes you think if Mira will show up for her shift, if Tim will deliver the Hawaiian rolls—

You hear a dog growl.

You must return to the store, you must. If a hurricane did this, or a busted water heater, insurance would cover the mess. Then again, the water heater exudes so much heat. God, its scalding. Maybe one of these boxes has Cabernets. Primitivos. A small dilemma burgeons in your head—should I or shouldn't I?

You hear either a gramophone or ole Harbi howling. One or the other says, A riot broke out at a factory off such-and-such island, which has halted exports. Your mission, should you—

Something tugs your arm, which you interpret as needing to visit this island. If the Doritos come from there, then Mira will have nothing to sell in the early morning hours. & so you run, & you run, & you didn't know you could run on water, but a waveless ocean lies beneath you. & you run, & you must be heading south, because your skin's on fire. You don't think about the lack of sun or the lack of wind, because it's getting harder to focus. You don't think that ole Harbi couldn't be barking, because your father euthanized him after he blindly slipped into the pool & nearly drowned, or maybe because he bit your sister's forearm & now she never leaves the house without elbow length gloves. You don't think that even if you find this factory, & get past the rioting screamers, that you won't have enough hands to haul multiple cases back to the store. You don't think you'll be trapped on that island, like a signal bottled when your dendrites are severed, not allowing for an SOS. You don't think about the sewer or the shotgun or how maybe ole Harbi got left with the luggage, under the plane, & insurance wouldn't cover the loss.

But it's hot, and it's—

II

Motivational Runner

Should she have taken a left on Monarch? Penny supposes all that matters is she clocks ten miles. A man in his burgundy bathrobe wheels out his trashcan, parks it near the curb. Must work from home, she thinks, then waves. He misses the gesture & the moment evanesces. Nothing wrong with inserting a little variety into the route; honestly, that's why she chose not to train on a treadmill. Could you imagine running in that sterile environment for hours? The only thing worse would be having to share a bathroom with Tabitha. Oh wait, she temporarily does, & is treated to yoga in front of the bathroom mirror. No earthly idea why she won't stretch outside with the goats. Stop, focus. If you twist your ankle in a pothole, your training for this half marathon is over. Is it Black Swallowtail that has the picturesque houses? She'd love to own one of those periwinkle paneled homes with the three-quarter porch. If only she could prod _____ into proposing, they could place an offer. Yes, that one there. Maybe she should screen shot it. Ugh, of course it's blurry. Well she's not circling back with eight miles to go. Honestly there's no point in Snapchatting him anyway, because he only applied for that office job when she suggested it, & he'd never buy a ring if she didn't pick it out, & he'd never—

Stop. Training for this marathon is all about positive energy. Focus on how blisteringly hot it is for June, not that it would've been cooler if you had started at 8:15, but Tabitha was doing the Bridge Pose while you brushed your teeth. Okay, focus on the burn in your calves, & not the fact that _____ burns the chicken every time he demands to grill. Let's go live. Feed off my subscribers, feeding off me pushing through limits. She checks herself in the screen's gloss—a cute sports bra, bright college tank top, hair—well. An amber alert pops up, but she swipes it away before skimming the notification, pulls up Instagram. Five. Four. Three. Hey guys, Penny here on mile three; just jogging down Juniper Hairstreak; sorry the hair's a mess, but transformations are rarely poised—

She did not just say that cheesy shit. Fuck. Behind her, blue jays dive-bomb into rooftops & windowpanes. Maybe nobody watched. Quick, how do you delete a post? & of course Brenda already commented: Looking great, Penny. Well it's staying up now. Let's take a right. Even if it adds a mile, she'll need it after this social annihilation. Remember, think of those runs for cancer, think of—honestly that narrative theory class was incomprehensible. Who has any idea who's telling their story & for what purpose? She lost sleep over that class, dates with _____ over that class. The day of the final, she hadn't slept, hadn't showered, honestly wasn't even sure if she tested in the proper language. So afterward she invited some friends to the bar, Brenda being one of them. Or was she invited by one of them? Either way, Shots. Toast: Here's to telling your own story! Shot after shot after shot. & yes when ordering some chill cheese fries, she might've spewed vomit across the bar top, but did that mean Brenda had to capture it on Instagram? Freaking social Armageddon. Nobody wants to see chunks of your failure splattered all over their newsfeed. It doesn't matter. Months of rebranding her image are in the past like that dog poop a mile back. No smell. No victory.

Shit. How hard is it to keep a shoelace tied? Let's just subtract ten seconds. Who's to know? Nobody said anything about that house not watering their hay-grass for months. Honestly how could anyone survive with such a shabby front? What does it matter. Just a few more miles. A silver Jag burns rubber during a ninety-degree drift; as it screeches past Penny, sunlight shimmers off its chrome rims. Remember to bring sunglasses next time. Oh & Airpods too. Well, she would've brought them had they had a chance to charge, but Tabitha unplugged them to power her Mac. Vlogging yoga. To be an only child. It's okay. Just create your own rhythm. One, two. One, two. No, too military. A civil-defense siren blares in the distance, but is obscured by a squall before reaching the suburbs. Hey, isn't that ole Nap's convenience store? Wow, she remembers getting her first Snoballs during fish camp for marching band. Her section leader had brought her there before the afternoon session as a team-building / bonding strategy. Nap's always commanded a full parking lot. If only _____ had the kind of conviction to spearhead his own enterprise. Instead, he's content slinging drinks for some other man. Hell, maybe it's time to call it off. Get that house on my own. Rosie across the street got hers on her own. Forget about recessions & mortgage rates. Running partner's nice & all, but maybe it's time to run the narrative— holy hell, *that* guy can sprint. Not the best form, but man can he move. Gross, he's puking what, a Bloody Mary? Bet Brenda would be all over that: puke some more honey, get a little lower, a few chunks in your hair, perfect; this is the you they've been dying to see.

I

Trauma Counselor

After flinging her wet hair forward, Tabitha wraps & twists a towel into a honeycomb. Her Mac has powered up. Keep things chipper, she tells herself, but her peripherals catch a whiff of brown boxes stacked in the corner, which given the morning's nascent, forces a frown. Creases, she tells herself, creases, then smiles into the webcam. Hello y'all, Tabitha here, & I'm sure most of you tuned in for this week's tips on organic snacks that help improve brain health, with those finals looming closer, maybe for some of you those quarterly reports are due, or maybe you tuned in for a sneak peek at next week's best Spring outfits for matching your miniature dog, but sadly my sister (who moved back yesterday, because she got laid off from work), woke me up early to utterly ruin my entire week, & I actually could use some advice. As some of you might remember, the big writer's conference happens this weekend, & I've looked forward to it so much because it's actually within driving distance this year, but rumors are circulating online that up to half of the publishing houses & keynote speakers are considering cancelling. A little more digging (which wasn't really necessary, because my sister highlighted it in teal), showed that some cruise ship guests had gotten too drunk (or caught the flu), & were making an extra vacation stop on a military base within relative proximity to the convention center. The schedule hasn't been updated on all the cancellations or possible cancellations so missing certain lectures can't be a tipping point, but should I still miss work for this convention? Booty2Bumble I'm not sure if this cruise ship visited China or not; what should it matter?

We're in Texas. Thank you DogsRPeople for your kind words; regardless of my decision, you'll still get those tips when & if I return. My parents (bless their souls), already think we're both squandering too much money on this degree, & this conference is a way to legitimize all our hard work, & the booths promote their upcoming contests, so maybe a potential break. SpringBreak4Life people in your town are hording toilet paper & face masks? Well the mummy look isn't resurrecting in fashion, & a facemask would muzzle a small dog. TerryLikesBass you've heard rumors on Twitter that a musical festival might be cancelled too? & you think they're connected? Y'all we've survived Category five hurricanes, & black mold in my grandmother's entire house, even had to toss that antique wooden paneling she loved so much, Jesus, her wedding dress, & there weren't any toilet paper shortages, or worries of secondhand hangovers. Wouldn't you bet that with an election approaching, there's some conspiracy circulating, some Boogeyman with the sniffles? Pollen's in the air, people! Just pop a Claritin. Might have to get back into yoga, because it's all about a holistic approach. We really must remember to prioritize what's important. My laptops battery's dying, but thank you for all the words of encouragement & insights. I'm sure anyone who skips this conference will look back a year from now, & see what hysteria caused them to miss. My sister needs the room to Facetime her dead-beat boyfriend, oh sorry you heard that? But I wanted to leave y'all with this inspirational quote from my favorite poet that said: no wait, hey, give me back my Mac; I'm not finished yet

NOTES

"Six by Infinity" – The title references the measurement of space between the two people.

"A Night in Venice" – The poem is loosely based on my trip to Venice in the summer of 2015.

Obi & the monster commune are the byproduct of a D&D styled writing exercise done in a hybrid workshop.

John Berryman's "Dream Songs" referenced (in order of appearance): 14, 264, 367, 223.

(.. ..-. / -.-- --- ..- / ..-. --- -.-. ..- ...) is Morse Code for "if you focus."

The four bronze horses at the entrance of St. Mark's Basilica were placed there after the sack and looting of Constantinople in 1204.

The building sunk just outside of Piazza Saint Marco is in the 2006 film, Casino Royale.

"Spin Cycle" – In 2017, internet memes portrayed Tide Pods (laundry capsules) as delicious food, mocking those that had accidentally mistaken the colorful wrapping for an edible treat. In early 2018, the viral memes playfully led to a Tide Pod Challenge (like the Gallon Challenge or Cinnamon Challenge), where teens would film themselves intentionally swallowing a Tide Pod, then daring their friends to accept the challenge. The result was the American Association of Poison Control Centers reporting additional poison cases and deaths.

"Fine Dining after a Draught out of Rip's Flagon" – The title is an allusion to the last line of Washington Irving's "Rip Van Winkle."

"A Bed of Bees" – When this collection was originally envisioned as a chapbook, this was to be the title.

The opening lines of The Canterbury Tales & "The Waste Land" are alluded to.

"Call Me Bonzo" – Bonzo is John Bonham's nickname, the historic drummer of Led Zeppelin.

"Minute Maid Cadence" – The Houston Astros won the World Series in 2017. A couple years later an ex-Astros pitcher blew the whistle on how the team had stolen pitching signs using trashcan lids & cameras, thus bringing into question the legitimacy of their title.

Othello Act 2.3.356.

"What do we say to the god of death?" – The title is a quote from Game of Thrones. The proper response is "not today."

On May 9, 2019, a petition was created on change.org to "recreate Game of Thrones Season 8 with competent writers." At the time of writing this note, 1,860,614 angry fans have signed the petition.

"A Red Pill" – An allusion to the 1999 film, The Matrix.

"The Art of Going Green" – "what's in a name?" An allusion to Romeo & Juliet Act 2.2.46.

"The Forever Spring Break" – On January 24, 2019, Business Insider released an article titled "7 times people thought the world was going to end."

"Pneumonoultramicroscopicsilicovolcanoconiosis"–"P45" is shorthand for title; Deal or No Deal is a 2000's gameshow.

"Stocking up on the Essentials" – A golden shovel based on Pink Floyd's "Brain Damage."

"Death, Contagion & Unnatural Sleep" – The title is an allusion to Romeo & Juliet Act 5.3.157.

"Gee Brain, what are we gonna do tonight?" – Pinky & the Brain is a 1990's cartoon show that chronicles the attempt of two lab rats to take over the world.

"The Art of Going Extinct" - Yangtze Sturgeon & Pinta Giant Tortoise are two species that had recently gone extinct at the time of writing this poem.

"A Case for Icarus" – The two poems alluded to are "Landscape with the Fall of Icarus" by William Carlos Williams & "Musée des Beaux Arts" by W.H. Auden.

"When Hamlet has Insomnia" – a meditation on the Act 3.1.74-82 segment of Hamlet's "To be or not to be" soliloquy.

In 2020, due to the COVID-19 pandemic, MLB postponed Opening Day till July 23, condensing the 162-game season to 60 games.

"Estimated Time of Arrival" – In February 2020, Bored Panda released an article "21 Bizarre Medical Practices Used In The Past That Will Make You Appreciate Modern Medicine."

Acknowledgments

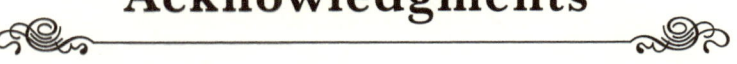

First and foremost, I want to thank Kurt Loveless and the **Pierian Springs Press** for believing in this collection enough to bring it to life.

I would like to thank the *Academy of American Poets* for previously publishing "A Bed of Bees" as a winner of the **2020 William C. Weathers Memorial Prize**.

I want to extend my extreme gratitude to Scott Kaukonen, Katie Jean Shinkle, and Nick Lantz for their invaluable mentoring during and beyond my MFA at **Sam Houston State University**.

In keeping with Sam Houston, I want to thank my fellow graduate students who read and advised on multiple versions of these poems. I reiterate—multiple versions.

To my **Hidden Cellar** family, thank you for your constant support.

To my mom, dad, and the rest of my family, thank you for your love and patience.

About the Author

Tyler Deaton

Tyler Deaton has an MFA in creative writing. He is a poet and a novelist. Tyler won the *2020 William C. Weather Memorial Prize* for his poem "A Bed of Bees" which is up on the *Academy of American Poets* site. OF DEATH, CONTAGION & UNNATURAL SLEEP is Tyler's debut collection of poetry.